Teen
FAQ
Keeping Healthy

Teen FAQ

Keeping Healthy

Anne Rooney

ARCTURUS

This edition first published in 2010 by Arcturus Publishing
Distributed by Black Rabbit Books
P.O. Box 3263
Mankato, Minnesota 56002

Printed in China

Planned and produced by Discovery Books Ltd.
www.discoverybooks.net
Managing editor for Discovery Books: Rachel Tisdale
Editors: Clare Collinson and Rachel Minay
Designer: D. R. ink
Consultant: Xanthe Fry, School Counselor and Educational Consultant
Picture researcher: Rachel Minay

Library of Congress Cataloging-in-Publication Data

Rooney, Anne.
  Keeping healthy / Anne Rooney.
     p. cm. -- (Teen FAQ)
  Includes bibliographical references and index.
  ISBN 978-1-84837-705-9 (library binding : alk. paper)
  1. Teenagers--Health and hygiene--Juvenile literature. I. Title.
  RA777.R65 2011
  613'.0433--dc22
                              2010012716

Picture credits
Corbis: 8 (moodboard), 9 (David Stoecklein), 12 (moodboard), 13 (Image Source), 21 (Louisa Gouliamaki/epa), 27 bottom (Creasource), 31 (Vincent Hazat/PhotoAlto). Getty: cover (Reggie Casagrande/The Image Bank), 16 (Jupiterimages), 20 (Blasius Erlinger), 29 (Purestock), 32 (Yellow Dog Productions), 33 (Zia Soleil), 35 (Gary Gershoff/Stringer). Istockphoto.com: 17 (Travis Manley), 22, 30 (Chris Price), 43 (Jeanell Norvell). Science Photo Library: 14 (AJ PHOTO), 42 (CC STUDIO). Shutterstock: 6 (Galina Barskaya), 7 (Mandy Godbehear), 10 (Elena Schweitzer), 11 (Monkey Business Images), 15 (thumb), 18 (T-Design), 19 (Galina Barskaya), 23 (Netfalls), 25 bottom (Christo), 25 top (Factoria singular fotografia), 27 top (Monkey Business Images), 28 (Laurence Gough), 34 (Losevsky Pavel), 36 (Adam Tinney), 37 (David Davis), 38 (Daniel Rajszczak), 40 (Fresnel), 41 (empipe).

SL001459US
Supplier 03, Date 0510

Contents

1 How can I stay healthy?

How are you feeling? Are you full of energy, cheerful, enthusiastic, and ready to get the most from life? Or are you tired, run-down, miserable, grumpy, and under the weather? Living healthily can make all the difference to how you feel—not just whether you are well or sick, but also whether you are enthusiastic and optimistic and enjoy life.

Exercise can be great fun as well as being good for you.

What is a healthy lifestyle?

Keeping healthy involves many areas of everyday activity. It includes diet (what you eat), exercise and fitness, and your daily routine. But it's not just about physical behavior. It also includes your emotional well-being, the relationships you have with friends and family, and keeping yourself safe from sickness, injury, and trauma.

Feeling comfortable with your looks boosts your confidence and **self-esteem**—and that makes you look even better!

DO YOU LIKE YOUR BODY?

Many young people are not happy with their bodies for one reason or another. A recent study found that 53 percent of American girls are "unhappy" with their bodies at age 13 and 78 percent at age 17.

How can I get healthier?

Dear Agony Aunt,
I think I might be a bit on the chubby side and I get out of breath easily if I do any exercise. I also seem to be tired a lot of the time. I'd like to lose a bit of weight and have more energy and just enjoy life more. What should I be doing to make things better for myself?
Carrie, 16

Dear Carrie,
The fact that you want to make changes to your lifestyle is a great start. You say you might be overweight and you don't have much energy, so you probably need to do more exercise. It may seem strange, but doing exercise will give you more energy, and getting fit will mean you have more energy all of the time. You will find it easier if you find a type of exercise you really enjoy—this could be dancing with friends, walking a neighbor's dog, or joining a class such as aqua aerobics or badminton. Also check that you eat a healthy diet (see pages 10–17). And have fun! Spending time with people who make you feel good and using your leisure time properly—not just slouching in front of the TV or computer—will help you to get the most from life.

What is health?

"Health" is not the same state for everyone—it is very individual. For most people, being free of disease or injury, having all the energy they need, and being happy counts as being healthy. For a top-level athlete, the health and fitness barrier is set higher than for most people, and for an elderly and infirm person it may be set lower.

When you are in good health, your body works efficiently, you don't easily pick up minor infections such as colds and mouth ulcers, and you have lots of energy. Minor injuries will heal quickly and your body will grow and develop as it should for your age. You are more likely to feel cheerful and optimistic if you are fit and healthy, too.

IT HAPPENED TO ME

I get bad **asthma** and I've always been too scared to do a lot of **strenuous** activity in case I have an asthma attack. But last year I got a new sports teacher at school and she explained that doing some exercise will actually improve my lung function. She told me to take up a wind instrument or singing to help develop my lung function gently. So now I play the clarinet and it really has helped my asthma. I do quite a lot of sports now—I just make sure I always have my inhalers and stop if I start feeling wheezy. I feel so much better—I have more confidence and much more energy now that I join in with sports.

Christopher, 14

Many medical conditions are easily kept under control and don't need to interfere with a healthy lifestyle.

It's important to keep fit even if you have a disability—don't let it stop you enjoying sports or exercise.

"I want to see more disabled and non-disabled children . . . become more active in sport . . . There is so much to be gained from taking part in sport in terms of health, well-being, and enjoyment of life."

Gregory Campbell, Sports Minister, UK

LOOK AFTER YOURSELF

Teenagers with disabilities are more likely than others to smoke, eat a poor diet, or have an inactive lifestyle.

Health and disability

Some people live with disability or a **chronic** illness. This does not mean that they cannot be healthy in all other regards. Indeed, if you have an ongoing condition, it is especially important to look after your health as you may be at more risk than other people.

Many people take medication, undertake **physiotherapy,** or take some other form of treatment on a regular basis. Taking medication as **prescribed,** or attending treatment sessions, is part of a healthy routine and forms the basis of good health. If you have a disability, you may need to work a little bit harder than some of your friends to stay healthy—but it is well worth the effort as you will be happier and get more out of life if you are fit and healthy.

2 What is a healthy diet?

Food is fuel for the body. Your body breaks down food to get energy for activities and to maintain essential functions such as breathing. It also needs food to grow, repair itself after injury and sickness, and to stay healthy.

Food groups

Bread, cereals, rice, pasta, and potatoes are starchy foods. They contain a lot of starchy **carbohydrates** and should form the main part of each meal. Carbohydrates are a source of energy for the body, and provide fibre and vitamin B. Fruit and vegetables provide fibre, vitamins, and minerals, and should make up another large part of your diet. Fibre keeps your bowel working well. Vitamins and minerals are needed to keep the body healthy. **Deficiencies** of particular vitamins and minerals are associated with serious diseases.

Meat, fish, and beans are good sources of protein. Protein is needed to build and repair the body. Oily fish, such as mackerel and salmon, contain unsaturated fats, which are good for the body—try to eat these once or twice a week.

Keep fatty, sugary, and salty foods to a minimum.

Starchy foods and fruit and vegetables should make up the main part of your daily food intake. You need protein, too—but keep less healthy treats to a minimum.

What should I eat?

Dear Agony Aunt,
I've been feeling run down, and my girlfriend said I should eat a healthier diet. My mom doesn't eat very healthily, though. We always eat takeout and burgers and french fries, and don't often have any vegetables or fruit. So I don't know where to start. Do you have any advice?
Adam, 15

Dear Adam,
A healthy diet is a balanced diet. That means that you need to eat the right proportions of different types of nutrients. It's easier to work out what to eat if you think of foods in terms of different groups. You need to eat the right balance of carbohydrates, fibre, and protein. You should keep sugary and fatty foods to a minimum. Try and encourage your mom to eat more healthily, too. Why not cook a family meal of pasta and sauce with vegetables for your mom? Perhaps she will see how tasty healthy food can be.

Five a day

Eat at least five **portions** of fruit and vegetables a day. Fruit and vegetables contain vitamins and minerals that your body needs, as well as fibre, which helps bowel activity and can help regulate the level of sugar in the blood. Eating fruit and vegetables will also cut your risk of **coronary heart disease** and some kinds of cancer. You can include fresh, frozen, dried, canned, and juiced versions. To preserve the vitamins, eat them raw or lightly cooked, and keep the peel on if possible.

HEALTH WARNING

Some people take food supplements or vitamin pills hoping to stay healthy, but the body may not absorb some nutrients from supplements as easily as from real foods. Supplements do not contain everything the body needs. Unless advised by your doctor, a balanced diet is better than a handful of pills.

Fresh fruit is not only good for you—it makes a delicious snack.

CALORIES

The energy content of food or the energy we expend in activity is measured in calories or kilojoules (1 calorie = 4.2 kJ). Scientists work out the energy content of food by burning food in controlled conditions and measuring the heat released by using it to heat up a known volume of water. A calorie is the amount of energy needed to raise the temperature of 1 gram (0.04 oz.) of water by 1 degree Celsius (1.8°F).

Cut back

Fatty and sugary foods, such as chocolate, potato chips, cakes, cookies, and pastries, contain lots of "empty calories"—energy with very little nutritional benefit for the body. Eating too much of this food group can lead to weight gain and also increases the risk of heart disease and cancer. However, eating small amounts of treat foods within a balanced diet will not hurt you.

You should avoid eating lots of salty foods, or adding a lot of salt to your food, as too much salt can lead to several medical problems including high blood pressure, kidney disease, and **strokes**.

Good fat, bad fat

Fats provide energy for the body, but you don't need very much. Most people eat too much fat. It is found in foods such as butter, cheese, margarine, ghee, oils, fatty meat, and many **processed foods**.

Young people who live with adults who are overweight are more likely to become overweight or obese themselves.

Fats may be saturated or unsaturated. Saturated fats, found in dairy products and red meat, are more harmful than unsaturated fats. Processed meat products, such as sausages, often contain very high levels of saturated fat, so eat these rarely. Trim visible fat off any meat you eat. Unsaturated fats are good for you in small amounts. Foods containing unsaturated fats include oily fish, avocados, and sunflower and olive oils.

Too much and too little

It is important to eat the right quantity of food. If you eat too much, the body stores energy as fat—that's why overeating leads to weight gain. On the other hand, if you eat too little, you will be lacking in energy, more likely to get sick, and may even suffer from **malnutrition**. You may also develop malnutrition if you consume enough calories but do not have a balanced diet, and even some obese people suffer from malnutrition.

TEENAGERS' CALORIE REQUIREMENTS

Girls	Recommended average calories per day
11–14 years	1,845
15–18 years	2,100
Boys	**Recommended average calories per day**
11–14 years	2,220
15–18 years	2,755

A HEALTHY WEIGHT

Doctors often use BMI (body mass index) to check that someone is a healthy weight. To work out your BMI, divide your weight (in pounds) by your height (in inches) squared, and multiply by 703. Below 18.5 is underweight; 18.5–24.5 is normal weight; over 24.5 is overweight.

In addition, if your waist is larger than your hip measurement (boys) or is more than 0.8 times your hip measurement (girls), you need to lose weight.

Adding salt to food that is already high in saturated fat makes it even more unhealthy.

IT HAPPENED TO ME

I didn't set out to lose weight, but I wanted to be a better cross-country runner. I started eating less, and doing lots of extra gym sessions. As I lost weight, I found I could run faster, and people complimented me on how I looked. But I took it too far. Soon, I had no energy and struggled to run at all. My periods stopped—that's common when you're underweight—and I started to get infections all the time. I ate only a few mouthfuls of food a day. I was lucky—my mom noticed how thin and unhealthy I was, and made me see the doctor. With help from my mom and my doctor, I started to eat and soon gained weight. Now, three years on, I train every other day and am a good runner—and a healthy weight.

Isobel, 18

Young people who are a healthy weight but worry that they should be thinner are in danger of slipping into unhealthy eating habits and making themselves sick.

Eating disorders

Some young people develop an unhealthy attitude toward food, often tied up with poor body image (see pages 34–35). They may try to diet to lose weight, and some take this to extremes, developing an eating disorder such as anorexia nervosa or bulimia nervosa. Anorexics become obsessed with losing weight. They fall below a healthy weight and then often develop associated health problems. Bulimics often binge, eating large amounts of food, and then making themselves sick to get rid of the surplus food and avoid weight gain. Someone with an eating disorder often sees a fat person when he or she looks in the mirror, even if in reality that person is already dangerously thin.

Anorexia and bulimia are dangerous, even deadly, disorders and are difficult to treat. Treatment involves restoring the person to a healthy weight, dealing with the psychological issues behind the problem, and preventing the person continuing with, or returning to, poor eating habits, by addressing the actions and thoughts that lead to them.

HEALTH WARNING

Going on a weight-loss diet means restricting food intake so that your body burns stored fat. If you are overweight, you should lose weight to improve your health, but take advice from a doctor first. Your doctor will help you put together an eating plan that will be suitable for you and keep you healthy while you lose weight gradually but steadily. Rapid dieting can be dangerous, as you will first lose lots of water and then become weak, as your body does not have enough energy day-to-day. You will be vulnerable to sickness and injury, and you will actually lose weight more slowly than if you dieted sensibly, as your **metabolic rate** will slow down. Rapid dieting is rarely effective in the long term, and most people who go on "crash" diets put the weight back on quickly.

Is junk food really junk?

Junk food is often high in saturated fat, sugar, and salt. This is not good for your body, so you should not eat it often—but it's OK as an occasional treat. If you are eating out, it's better to choose steamed or grilled rather than fried food (steamed rice instead of fried rice, for instance). Choose pasta with a tomato sauce rather than a burger and fries, or grilled fish instead of fried chicken.

Many traditional diets are healthy—rich in vegetables and starchy carbohydrates. Meals cooked from scratch also tend to have fresh ingredients and far fewer chemical additives than many ready meals.

Special diets

Some people follow a special diet for religious or medical reasons or for reasons of personal belief or choice. It is quite easy to eat healthily if you are a vegetarian who eats dairy products and eggs. If you are vegan, you may have to be careful to get enough iron, calcium, vitamin D, and vitamin B12. Vitamin B12 is only found naturally in animal products, so you will need to eat foods that have had B12 added to them. A vegetarian diet is not automatically healthy—you still need to balance what you eat and make healthy choices.

Religious diets are generally as healthy as any other. If you are following a special diet for medical reasons, you should not vary it without taking advice from a doctor, as it will have been developed to be suitable for you.

Drinking

An adult needs around 5–7.5 pints (2.5–3.5 l) of fluid a day, and around a fifth of this usually comes from food. A younger and smaller person needs a bit less, but you will need more on a hot day or if you are exercising. You can drink your fluids as water, juice, milk, tea, coffee, and soft drinks—it doesn't have to be water. Always drink if you feel thirsty, otherwise your body may start to **dehydrate**. Drinking much more than you need is also bad for you, as the essential salts in your body are **diluted**.

Alcohol

Drinking alcohol in moderation is harmless for most adults, but is not recommended for younger people. Too much alcohol can lead to short-term problems such as drunkenness, a **hangover**, and accidents related to being drunk. It can also cause more serious problems, including liver disease, **alcohol poisoning**, and even death.

"People are choosing the vegetarian option thinking it's healthier when quite often the dish is full of carbs, sugars, salts, saturated fats, hydrogenated fats, and no worthwhile protein."

Zhou Qinglu, Nutritionist, Beijing Institute of Sport Science, China

HEALTH WARNING

It has long been known that drinking too much alcohol can lead to fatty liver disease—a build-up of fat tissue in the liver. Research in 2009 suggested that soda pop and fruit juice can have the same effect. Drinking more than 1 pint (0.5 l) of soda pop a day was found to increase the risk of fatty liver disease.

FAQ

3 Am I fit?

Being physically fit and active is an important aspect of health. If you are not fit, you are likely to have less energy and be unable to do all the things you want to do. Keeping fit can be fun—there are plenty of activities to choose from.

Aspects of fitness

Fitness involves stamina (the ability to keep going with an activity), flexibility (the bendiness of your body), and strength. Different types of activity build these different aspects of physical fitness, so it's a good idea to mix and match your sports and activities. Gymnastics and yoga are great for flexibility for example, while running is good for building stamina, and weight training helps develop strength. Swimming is an excellent all-around activity that helps build all three.

Exercise is good for you!

Exercise uses your muscles. This builds and maintains them. The more you use your muscles, the stronger they will be. Your heart is a muscle, and exercise makes your heart work, as it has to deliver oxygen-carrying blood to the rest of your body at a faster rate than usual. So exercise strengthens your heart, too, and protects you against heart disease in later life.

Exercise also helps to develop your lung capacity as you breathe more deeply and more rapidly to get the oxygen your body needs. As your blood is pumped around your body, it carries extra oxygen to your brain as well, making you more alert and improving your thinking skills and concentration.

Exercise also keeps you flexible—it's good for the soft tissues in your body—and it helps to strengthen your bones.

HOW MUCH EXERCISE SHOULD YOU DO?

U.S. guidelines suggest that teenagers should aim to do an hour of physical activity every day. This does not need to be an organized sport, though sports are often an easy and enjoyable way of getting exercise. It could include kicking or throwing a ball around with friends, cycling to school, swimming, ice-skating, or walking a dog.

Swimming is an excellent all-around exercise and there are swimming pools in most towns and cities.

IT HAPPENED TO ME

I always hated sports at school because I was never chosen for teams. I spent most of my free time watching TV and playing on my games console. But when I was 14 my uncle took me rock climbing. It was so cool! It didn't feel like exercise, but after I'd been a few times I found I had more energy and my arms and legs were stronger. I even enjoyed cycling and running around in the park. It really made a difference—I'm much happier and more relaxed now.

Craig, 15

Feel good and keep fit

Strenuous activity makes the brain release endorphins, chemicals which make you feel good. These produce the "high" that people often feel after about 20 minutes of activity. The good effects of exercise last long after you finish the activity. If you exercise regularly, you will soon feel more alert and energetic all of the time. Your concentration will improve and you will want to carry on being active. You will also control your weight, sleep better, and feel less stressed. If you are under pressure at school or because of exams, exercise can be just what you need to make you feel better.

Physical activity need not be a formal sport—running around with family or friends is also good exercise.

The contestants in the Paralympics achieve astonishing feats, far beyond the abilities of most able-bodied people.

HEALTH WARNING

Don't bow to pressure from a sports coach or team members to take **anabolic steroids** or other performance-enhancing drugs. Anabolic steroids, which are related to the male hormone **testosterone**, help to build muscle and to develop and maintain masculine characteristics such as beard growth. They can be bad for your body if misused—they can lead to liver damage, high cholesterol levels, and high blood pressure, for instance. If they are discovered in your system you are likely to be banned from taking part in your sport, and possibly even from training.

An active life

It is easy to build more activity into your daily life, and this will help you to keep fit and healthy. Try to walk, run, or cycle instead of going by car or bus, and use stairs instead of an elevator or escalator. If you meet up with friends, go skateboarding or swimming instead of using the computer, or dance at a gig instead of going to the movie theater.

Exercise and disability

If you have a disability, there is still plenty you can do. The Paralympics are an inspiring equivalent of the Olympic Games for athletes with disabilities. Athletes take part in all types of sporting events from basketball to skiing. Unless you are severely disabled, there should be a form of exercise to suit you.

4 Does my daily routine matter?

Some people like to live a very ordered life and others are quite chaotic and disorganized. Most of us are somewhere in between. Even if you don't like to follow a strict routine, you need to fit some time into your day to look after your body properly.

What do I need to do?

You probably already have a daily routine of personal hygiene that includes washing your body and your hair, brushing your teeth, and putting on clean clothes. It is easy to let some parts of this slip, though, as your life becomes busier. Yet a daily routine of hygiene is an important part of staying healthy. It only takes a few minutes each day, but helps to prevent problems such as bad skin, tooth decay, bad breath, and body odor.

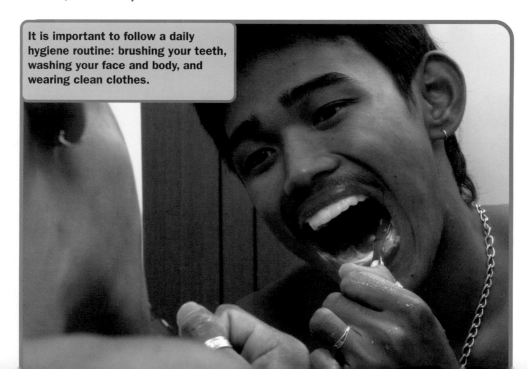

It is important to follow a daily hygiene routine: brushing your teeth, washing your face and body, and wearing clean clothes.

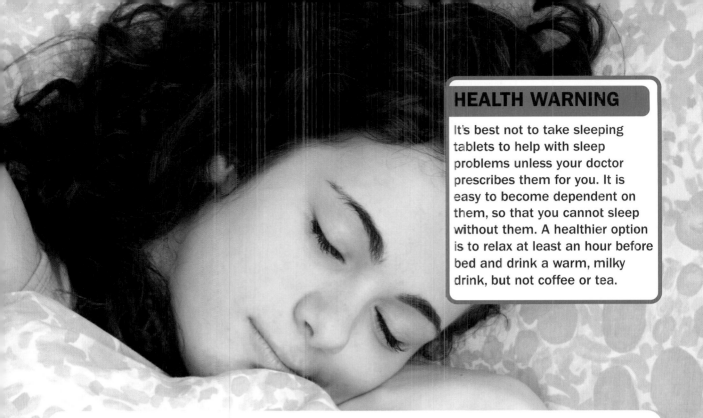

HEALTH WARNING

It's best not to take sleeping tablets to help with sleep problems unless your doctor prescribes them for you. It is easy to become dependent on them, so that you cannot sleep without them. A healthier option is to relax at least an hour before bed and drink a warm, milky drink, but not coffee or tea.

Help! I can't sleep

Dear Agony Aunt,
I have great difficulty sleeping and then I'm tired in the morning and really struggle to get up and go to school. My dad says I'm lazy but, really, I'm not. What can I do?
Henna, 15

Dear Henna,
Don't worry. I don't know any teenager who finds it easy to get out of bed in the morning! As you grow, your body clock shifts, and many young people find they are not tired in the evening and like to stay up late. As you will still have to get up for school that means you might not get enough sleep. Teenagers should ideally have eight and a half to nine hours of sleep a night.

Try to retrain your body to sleep earlier. Set a regular bedtime and stick to it, even if you don't feel sleepy. Avoid using the TV, computer, or a phone for an hour before bedtime, and do something relaxing such as having a warm bath or reading. Sleep in a dark room that is not too warm, but wake up to bright light. **Caffeine** (in coffee, tea, and cola), nicotine, and alcohol often keep people awake. It's best to avoid drinks containing caffeine for four hours before you go to bed. Stick to the routine at weekends or you will have difficulty getting to sleep on Sunday night.

I don't know how to tell my friend he has B.O.

Dear Agony Aunt,
My friend has a problem with body odor, but I don't think he is even aware of it. It has got worse over the last few months, and now people don't want to sit near him in class or on the bus. Someone should tell him, but I know he will be upset and embarrassed. What should I do?
Anand, 15

Dear Anand,
During puberty, the sweat glands become much more active and body odor is a problem for many teens, especially boys. Sweat does not smell itself—the smell is made by bacteria breaking down the sweat. Unfortunately, we aren't as aware of our own body odor as others are, so your friend may not know he has a problem unless someone tells him. One way to tell your friend is to buy him some shower gel and deodorant and say that you are using this brand—it's really good. If that doesn't work, or you want to be more direct, tell him gently that over the last few months you've noticed that he is sweating more. You could ask if he is worried about anything, as that can lead to increased sweating. Then mention that as a result his smell has changed, and you and some of his friends have noticed. Stress that you have worried about embarrassing him, but feel he should hear it from a friend. And then tell him that it's really easy to fix, just by washing each day, wearing clean clothes, and perhaps using a deodorant. It's a tricky thing to do, but he will probably thank you in the end.

"Teens don't want to smell . . . So many don't mind bathing and practicing good hygiene because they don't want people making fun of them at school."
Dr. Tanya Remer Altmann, Pediatrician, Mattel Children's Hospital at UCLA, California

All change

As young people move through puberty, their bodies change. Personal hygiene becomes more important, and it can sometimes seem quite a chore to keep up with it. Your body produces more sweat and oil, and you may find you need to wash more frequently and change your clothes more often to stay clean and fresh. Don't skip washing and don't cover up smells with deodorant or perfume—your body needs you to wash away the grime. If you have any parts of your body pierced, you need to clean these especially thoroughly, as it is easy for piercings to become infected.

As boys grow up, they need to add shaving to their daily routine.

Good habits

As they become older, boys will start to shave their beard hair, and many girls like to shave their underarms and legs. Keep razors clean and use them only when they are sharp to avoid cuts and infections.

Clean makeup off each night or you might develop skin problems, as makeup blocks the pores in your skin. Brush and wash out hairspray and styling products so that they don't build up on your hair, making it lank, dull, and sticky.

Removing any makeup before bed will help to keep skin clear and healthy.

FAQ

5 Happy and healthy?

Being happy and being healthy go hand in hand.
Emotional and mental well-being are closely linked
with physical health, and feeling good about yourself
is an important aspect of feeling good generally.
Having good self-esteem is vital if you are to be
healthy and happy.

Dealing with bullies

Bullying does not always involve physical violence. Being consistently
mean to someone, making unkind remarks or jokes they don't find
funny, and deliberately excluding people from activities and

My friends aren't nice to me

Dear Agony Aunt,
My school friends make me feel bad about myself. They call me "fatty" and laugh at my clothes. If I complain, they say I can't take a joke. And they often organize events and don't ask me to go. I don't have anyone else to do things with, though, so I don't want to drop them—otherwise I'd be on my own.
Ben, 15

Dear Ben,
Friends are people who are supportive and make you feel good, so these people are not acting like friends. Maybe they don't realize how unhappy this makes you. Tell them that you realize they are joking and mean no harm, but you don't like it. Maybe suggest an event or outing yourself so that you can invite them. If they still treat you badly, you'll need to look for other friends. There may be other people in your class or school who you have overlooked but who could become friends. You could also try joining a club, in or out of school, to do an activity that you enjoy or are good at. This is a great way of meeting new people and raising your self-esteem at the same time.

conversations is also bullying. If you are treated like this, you can ask your school for advice. The school will have an antibullying policy that gives guidance on dealing with the problem.

It is easy to be drawn into bullying behavior, or give approval to bullying by not speaking out against it. If your friendship group is bullying someone, perhaps excluding that person from activities or making fun of him or her, you are guilty if you encourage it, take part in it, or just stay silent. A school counselor or sympathetic teacher will help you to deal with this situation and talk with your friends about their behavior.

Spending time with people who value you and are supportive is good for your mental and emotional well-being.

Bullies often isolate their target and exclude him or her from group activities.

IT HAPPENED TO ME

I was at a very competitive school where all the teachers pushed us constantly to achieve good exam grades. I found the pressure too much. I'm not very academic and I was spending all my time trying to keep up. I became depressed because I felt all the time that whatever I did wasn't good enough, and soon I felt I wasn't a worthwhile person. Eventually I saw a counselor who advised that I move to a school that is better suited to my interests and abilities and less competitive. My parents agreed to let me change schools and I am much happier—I am doing lots of sports and music, which I really love, and my performance in academic subjects has improved.

Emma, 16

Balance

Working all the time is not good for you—you need time to relax and have fun as well as time to study. You will study more effectively if you balance your time between work and leisure.

Schoolwork and stress

Many teenagers feel under pressure to work hard and perform well at school. How well you do can affect your future plans, so it is understandable that many young people find the pressure intense. In some ways, stress can be good—it spurs you to do your best, and can give you a boost when you do well. But too much stress can make you unhappy and sick. Don't let worry about exams and schoolwork get out of proportion.

You need to work hard at school and for exams, but you will learn and concentrate better if you are generally healthy and take time to relax, too.

Getting out to relax and have fun will help to keep you happy and beat stress.

Relax!

Exercise and fresh air help you relax, so a brisk walk outside is a good instant stress-beater. You might find that sitting quietly listening to music, learning to play a musical instrument, or singing helps to reduce stress, too. Learning a relaxation technique, such as yoga, breathing exercises, or **meditation**, gives you a way to calm yourself down easily and quickly.

HEALTH WARNING

Stress not only makes you unhappy, it can also make you sick. If you are stressed all the time and can't relax, you may find it difficult to eat and sleep properly and may develop physical **symptoms** such as headaches, nausea, **panic attacks**, and backache. If stress makes you run down through lack of sleep and exercise, or poor eating habits, you will easily pick up viruses such as coughs and colds.

SELF-HARM

Some teens self-harm as a way of dealing with unhappiness or stress, using physical pain to distract them from mental pain. Self-harming is not a solution to underlying problems. Other ways of dealing with negative feelings are to keep a private diary, to draw or write about your feelings and then destroy the paper, to hit a pillow, or destroy something of no value (such as a newspaper). This lets your feelings out. Bouts of anger or wanting to harm yourself do not mean you are "mad" or have serious problems, but these are signs that things are difficult for you. Try to confide in a trusted adult, such as a teacher, doctor, or counselor. If you feel a real need to self-harm, there are safe ways to do it—by keeping a rubber band around your wrist (not too tight) and pinging it against the skin, or by holding ice cubes, for example. But self-harm is dangerous: you may get an infection, or hurt yourself more than you intend, so do seek help if you feel a strong desire to harm yourself.

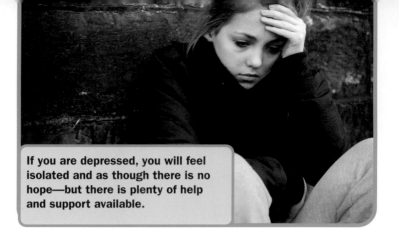

If you are depressed, you will feel isolated and as though there is no hope—but there is plenty of help and support available.

Depression

Depression may be mild, but can also be a serious mental illness. It is common to feel deeply unhappy for a few days when something bad happens—when you get a bad grade in an exam, or break up with a boyfriend or girlfriend, for example. If feelings of misery go on for more than a few days, or feelings of despair become overwhelming, it's time to seek help in case serious depression is taking a hold. If you are depressed, you may be unable to get up, unable to see any point in doing anything, and have very low self-esteem. Depression affects many teens and young people, as well as older people of both genders.

Identifying and dealing with depression

When you are depressed, you can't take pleasure in things you once enjoyed and can't motivate yourself to meet friends or do schoolwork. You may develop physical symptoms such as stomach problems, sleep problems, or headaches. If you suspect that you are suffering from depression, talk to a parent or guardian first. If they can't help, you should seek medical help. It is nothing to be ashamed of, so don't delay seeking help. Many successful people and celebrities have suffered from depression, and have been open about their problems and how they have dealt with them. You might find some of their stories encouraging or inspiring.

One of the symptoms of depression is, sadly, not feeling it is worth asking for help, as nothing can be done—but this is not true. There are several types of **therapy** and medication, and one of them will be right for you. Untreated serious depression rarely gets better quickly, so it's important to get help.

Why am I depressed?

Depression in young people may be caused by changing hormones in the body, or by a traumatic event, such as a death in the family, divorce, or moving schools. Occasionally depression is caused by a chemical imbalance in the brain that may need ongoing medication to help maintain a normal balance. A trained psychiatric doctor will be able to diagnose the type of depression and choose a suitable treatment.

HEALTH WARNING

Untreated depression may get worse and lead to self-harm and even suicide. Suicide is the third most common cause of death in the 15–24 age group, and the fourth most common in the 10–14 age group. If you are having suicidal thoughts, seek help immediately. If you can't see a doctor right away, alert someone close to you, so that they will look after you. If you don't feel able to do that, call the National Suicide Prevention Lifeline (see page 45). The call is free.

A suicide attempt can be a tragic outcome of untreated teenage depression. Sometimes the person can be saved with medical help, but he or she may suffer lasting physical damage or disability.

6 Do girls and boys have different health issues?

Boys and girls can have some different health concerns during puberty. These may relate to personal hygiene, the changes brought about during puberty, or sexual health.

How girls change

Girls begin their periods during puberty, as well as growing more body hair and developing breasts. At first, periods may be irregular, but they usually settle down into a 21–35-day cycle. Some girls also find periods painful. To ease painful periods, a girl could try a natural remedy, such as a daily evening primrose oil or vitamin E tablet, holding a hot water bottle to her stomach or back, or taking an over-the-counter painkiller. If a girl's periods are particularly painful, a doctor may prescribe stronger painkillers. With all remedies and painkillers it is very important to follow the directions on the bottle or packet.

People grow and develop at different rates—it really doesn't matter if you are bigger or smaller than your friends, as long as you are healthy.

Exercise is very good for you, but as teens sweat more than children, you will need to shower after taking part in sports.

CHECK YOURSELF

Because men and women have different bodies, they are at risk of some different cancers, even at a young age. Young men should learn to check their testicles for signs of **testicular** cancer, which is most common in males aged 15–35. Young women, similarly, should learn to check their breasts for changes that might indicate breast cancer. Breast cancers are rare in young women, but it is important that a girl learns to check herself regularly.

Don't be embarrassed about feeling your body to do this—it is a healthy and sensible thing to do. You can get a leaflet from your doctor, or look in a book or on a reputable web site (see page 45) to find out how to do it.

How boys change

During puberty, a boy grows more body hair, his voice breaks, his body shape may change, and his skin changes, producing more oils and sweat. This means that boys can easily develop body odor unless they wash frequently. Hair usually becomes greasier, too, and may need to be washed more frequently. The need to shave regularly later in puberty adds another task to the daily routine.

IMAGES OF OURSELVES

In a survey carried out in 2009, only 27 percent of Australian teens said they are happy with their bodies. Half said that unhealthy body images are depicted positively in society and a third knew someone who has had an eating disorder, or have had one themselves.

How do you look?

Young people often become very preoccupied with appearance. They may spend more time and money on clothes, hair, or makeup, and worry if they get a spot or skin complaint. This is normal—but a few people take it to extremes. There is a huge amount of pressure to look good, and it can be easy to feel inadequate or develop low self-esteem if you feel you don't look as good as you would like to.

Media images

Magazines, posters, and movies are full of images of people who look impossibly beautiful. In fact, they *are* impossibly beautiful—most of these images have been enhanced using computers. If you aim to look like one of these icons of beauty, you are bound to be disappointed, because no one actually looks like that in real life.

Young people can easily become preoccupied with their appearance and strive after an impossible ideal.

Love your body shape

Clothes are often modelled by "size zero" models—very thin women who in some cases are unhealthy. This leads many teenage girls to become dissatisfied with their bodies, even if they are a healthy shape and weight. Teenage boys, too, can be affected by images of the perfect male body and by male models. They may try to slim to make their muscles more visible, or work out excessively to develop a muscly body. We all have our own natural body shape—some people are naturally slimmer than others—and all body shapes can be equally attractive. The secret to feeling good about your body is to find a style that suits you and shows off your best features.

Concern about eating disorders within the fashion industry has led some designers and magazines to choose larger models. There was huge public support when *Glamour* magazine showed a nude image of size 12 model Lizzie Miller (pictured) that had not been manipulated by computer software.

IT HAPPENED TO ME

When I was 14, I became completely obsessed with my appearance. I wouldn't go out of the house without spending an hour on my hair and makeup. It ruled my life, and it didn't even make me happy, as I never felt I looked good enough. My friends spent less time on their appearance and always seemed to look better than I did. Eventually my older sister told me I was wasting my time and money, as I looked beautiful with less makeup. She persuaded me to cut down my makeup time, and surprisingly I did feel better about my looks, and now I am genuinely happy with my appearance.

Mehreen, 17

STIs

STIs—or sexually transmitted infections—are conditions that are passed on during sexual intercourse and other types of sexual activity, often in body fluids such as semen and vaginal secretions. Condoms offer protection against many types of STI, but not all. Genital herpes is a common STI that can be passed on through skin-to-skin contact, and pubic lice (also called "crabs") are passed on through close contact, or sharing infested towels or bedding. Using a condom does not offer protection against pubic lice or herpes.

Anyone who has had unprotected sex should have a checkup at a doctor's office or special clinic that deals with STIs. Most STIs can be treated easily and effectively if spotted early, but many lead to more serious conditions if ignored. **Chlamydia**, for example, is an STI that often has no symptoms in women, but can lead to infertility if it is not treated. There is a very simple test for chlamydia, which everyone who is sexually active should have regularly—each year, or on changing sexual partners. It is also possible to pick up chlamydia at birth, so have a test even if you are not sexually active.

Some STIs can be passed on by different types of sexual activity or by contact with another person's body fluids, such as saliva from the mouth. It is better to have occasional health checks than to allow a condition to go undetected and untreated.

Once you have a serious boyfriend or girlfriend, you may need to start thinking about sexual health issues.

Sexual health

Many young people become sexually active in their late teens, so sexual health is another new aspect of health to think about. Sexual activity puts people at risk of sexually transmitted infections (STIs). The best way to avoid pregnancy and STIs is, of course, not to engage in any sexual activity. But if you are sexually active, using a condom will help to protect you against both pregnancy and STIs. There are also many other methods of contraception. Some people choose to use more than one, because methods such as the contraceptive pill or injection, and the cervical cap or intrauterine devices do not offer protection against STIs.

It is strongly recommended that girls have a vaccination before they become sexually active, to help protect them against **cervical cancer** caused by the HPV (Human Papilloma Virus) which can be transmitted through unprotected sex. Around 4 million cases of STIs in teens are reported each year in the USA.

Should I do it?

Dear Agony Aunt,
My boyfriend wants me to have sex with him, but I'm not ready. He says everyone does it, and if I refuse that it proves I don't love him. I don't want to lose him—what should I do?
Grace, 16

Dear Grace,
If you are not ready to have sex, don't—you may regret it later, feel used, and resent your boyfriend. He should not try to persuade you to do something you don't want to do—and if he loves you he will not blackmail you like this! Explain how you feel about him and about having sex. It is not true that "everyone" does it—it is a personal choice for each couple. If he really persists or tries to force you into having sex with him, he is bullying you and you should protect yourself by ending the relationship.

Pregnancy

A young woman who becomes pregnant accidentally should confirm the pregnancy as soon as possible so that she can decide what to do next. Doctors and sexual health clinics offer free pregnancy tests, and drug stores or pharmacies sell home test kits. If a young woman decides to continue with the pregnancy, it is important to learn about health in pregnancy. If a young woman wants to terminate the pregnancy (also called abortion), she will need medical help and accurate information. The law relating to termination varies between countries.

Some women who realize they have had sex without protection (either with no contraception or if the condom burst) use emergency contraception, usually the "morning after pill." It can be taken up to 72 hours after unprotected sex, but it's best to take it within 24 hours. The emergency pill is available from a doctor, sexual health clinic, and from some pharmacies and emergency departments. It is not an alternative to taking proper precautions, by using a regular method of contraception.

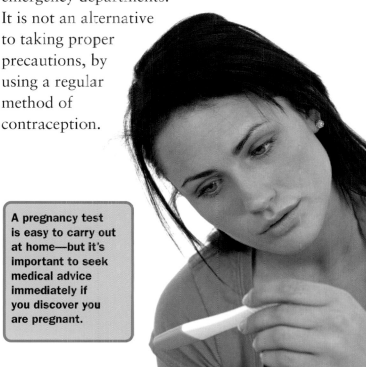

A pregnancy test is easy to carry out at home—but it's important to seek medical advice immediately if you discover you are pregnant.

7 How can I look after myself?

Looking after your health includes keeping yourself safe from sickness and injury. This means having regular medical checkups and following safety guidelines in any activities that might be risky.

Check it out

You should regularly go to the dentist and the optician to have your teeth and eyes tested. For most people, a dental checkup should be every six months and an eye test every one to two years, but your dentist or optician will tell you if you should go less or more frequently. If you do have any sight problems, getting glasses or contact lenses of the right prescription will make life more comfortable and help to protect you against eye strain and headaches. The optician will also check that your eyes are healthy. The dentist will check that your teeth and gums are healthy, give you advice about dental hygiene, and organize any dental treatment you may need.

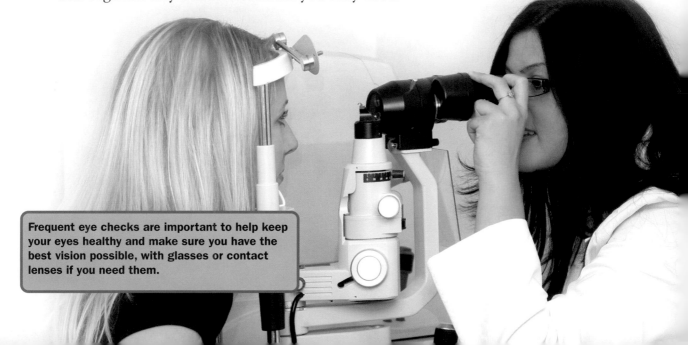

Frequent eye checks are important to help keep your eyes healthy and make sure you have the best vision possible, with glasses or contact lenses if you need them.

Do I have to have braces?

Dear Agony Aunt,
My dentist says I need braces but I don't want to have them. I think they look ugly, and I'd be scared of kissing girls. Also, I don't want to have to stop playing the trumpet. Are braces really necessary?
Karl, 16

Dear Karl,
Only your dentist can tell you whether they are truly necessary in your case. Orthodontic treatment is not always to make you look better. If your teeth are crowded or crooked, they may be more difficult to brush. Getting them straightened may save you from later tooth decay or teeth breaking under the strain of pushing against each other. If you do need braces, you will still be able to play the trumpet, though it will take a bit of practise. You can still kiss girls, and you can still look good.

Self-check

There are some problems you can be on the lookout for yourself. As well as checking for testicular or breast cancer (see page 33), you should keep an eye on any moles or skin irregularities you have. If a mole changes shape, bleeds, itches, or hurts, you should have it checked by a doctor, as it can be an early sign of skin cancer. Look out, too, for any odd blemishes, lumps, or rashes that do not go away. In general, if you notice any unusual changes in your body you should have them checked. Most of the time they will be harmless, but any condition caught early is easier to treat than if it is left to become established.

SAFETY IN THE SUN

Sunshine and fresh air are good for you, and you need some sunlight for your body to make vitamin D. But if you go out in the sun, you need to protect your skin from burning. Sunscreen and covering up with light clothing and a sunhat will keep you safe. Sunburn increases the risk of developing melanomas (skin cancer) later in life. Using a tanning bed to get a tan is particularly dangerous, as the damaging ultraviolet light is concentrated.

"Unfortunately the belief that a suntan is healthy is a myth. A suntan is the skin's response to damage from UV radiation—from sunlight or sunbeds ... The truth is that a suntan fades, but skin damage from tanning does not."

Dr. Annabel Bentley, Assistant Medical Director, Bupa

Regular hand washing cuts the risk of colds, flu, and stomach upsets.

DON'T START!

A survey in Canada in 2009 found that 70 percent of teens who smoke want to quit. Many young smokers first tried to quit after smoking for only two and a half months. Of those who had smoked for more than 12 months, only 19 percent succeeded in quitting.

Avoiding sickness

You can be protected against many serious diseases by having vaccinations. Make sure all your vaccinations are up-to-date, and get a booster shot if you need one.

It's easy to avoid many infections with some simple rules. Washing your hands regularly is one of the best defenses against infection, as many things we touch are swarming with disease-carrying **microbes**.

Preparing food hygienically, never using the same utensils or surfaces for cooked and uncooked foods, and throwing away food that is too old, will protect you against food poisoning.

Don't invite accidents

Safe behaviors, such as wearing a seatbelt in a car and a protective helmet when you use a bicycle or motorcycle, are essential. When taking part in sports or other activities, always follow safety guidelines, wear suitable clothing, and use protective equipment where necessary. Try to be aware of safety in other areas of your life, too. Even larking about—for example climbing and jumping off walls or play-fighting—causes many accidents, some of them fatal.

The risk of having an accident is much higher if you drink alcohol. Driving or cycling after drinking is very dangerous, and driving over the limit is illegal.

Safe living

Protect your health by avoiding risky behavior, such as drinking too much alcohol, smoking tobacco or marijuana, and taking non-medical drugs. If you already use any illegal substances, consider quitting —it can only be good for you.

It's sensible to wear a helmet when cycling. Cyclists who don't wear a helmet are 14 times more likely to die in an accident than cyclists who wear one.

FAQ

8 How can I get help?

There are lots of fads and trends in the coverage of health—so whose advice can you safely trust?

Reliable advice

If you look on the Internet for health advice, you will find some very reliable information, some biased advice, and some advice that is unreliable or wrong put up by individuals and organizations with a particular **agenda** or quirky enthusiasm. This can be dangerous. For example, lining up crystals on your body may do no harm, but doing this instead of seeking medical help for a genuine health problem could do a lot of harm. Trust advice only from a health professional such as a doctor or a school nurse. Online, you can usually trust web sites put up by national health organizations and major medical charities that deal with particular conditions such as cancer or diabetes, but they cannot diagnose your personal condition like a medical professional would.

SPEAK IN CONFIDENCE

Medical professionals have to respect patient confidentiality. They are not allowed to pass on anything you say to your parents or other people who are not professionally involved in your medical care without your permission, except in cases of real danger. So you are safe asking for help to quit smoking, asking for a pregnancy test, testing for an STI, or discussing other sexual issues without worrying that your parents will find out.

Medical professionals will not judge you or betray your confidence—it is always safe to ask for help or advice.

Support groups

There are many real-world and online groups that can offer you support with a health issue, such as quitting smoking, coping with a chronic illness, or motivating yourself to exercise. Remember that many of the suggestions on online forums are posted by non-experts, and you should not follow advice without checking with a medical professional, but the support of other people in the same position as you can be invaluable.

IT HAPPENED TO ME

I was depressed, and when I had a major row with my girlfriend I took an overdose. I didn't really want to die, though. I panicked and looked up what to do online. I found a site that said I didn't need to worry, I hadn't taken enough pills to die. But it turned out I had taken enough to suffer serious damage to my kidneys, and it took me a long time to get better because I didn't go straight to a hospital like I should have done.

Angela, 18

A support group can make it much easier to quit smoking or alcohol, as you quickly realize you are not alone with your struggle.

Glossary

agenda goals to be achieved or material to be dealt with

alcohol poisoning poisoning resulting from drinking a large amount of alcoholic drink, causing vomiting, confusion, unconsciousness, and sometimes liver damage, coma, or death

anabolic steroid a class of drug used to promote muscle growth

asthma a condition in which muscles in the lungs constrict, narrowing the small tubes in the lungs and making breathing difficult

caffeine a stimulant chemical found naturally in coffee, tea, cola and, to a lesser degree, chocolate

carbohydrate a chemical composed of carbon, oxygen, and hydrogen that may be either a starch or a sugar

cervical cancer cancer of the cervix—the neck of the womb

chlamydia a sexually transmitted bacterial disease which often has no symptoms in women, but can lead to infertility if untreated

chronic ongoing

coronary heart disease the failure of the heart and circulatory system to supply blood to the body; there are several possible causes

deficiency a lack of something that is essential

dehydrate to dry out

dilute to water down

hangover an aftereffect of consuming too much alcohol, often characterized by headache and nausea

malnutrition a medical condition that results from eating an inadequate diet over an extended period so that a shortage of essential nutrients leads to health problems

meditation the act of calming the mental state by controlled breathing, inactivity, and emptying the mind to induce a state of peacefulness

metabolic rate the rate at which the body uses energy in activities such as breathing, growing, pumping blood, and so on

microbe a microscopic organism or disease agent, such as a bacterium or virus

nutrient a chemical component of food that is needed by the body

orthodontic relating to correcting the bite or jaw alignment in dentistry

panic attack an extreme bout of anxiety accompanied by physical symptoms such as a racing heart, nausea, and disturbed breathing

physiotherapy physical activity designed to help correct a medical problem or heal an injury

portion an amount: one adult portion of fruit or vegetables is about 3 ounces (80 g); one child portion is roughly the amount that can be held in the palm of the child's hand

prescribed describing the supply authorized by a medical practitioner

processed foods foods that have been changed from their natural state by industrial processing, for example ready meals and ready-made sauces

self-esteem a person's belief in his or her own worth

strenuous requiring great effort

stroke a medical condition in which the blood flow to the brain is interrupted; it can lead to brain damage, disability, and death

symptom a physical or psychological problem or characteristic that is an indication of sickness

tendon tough body tissue that usually connects muscle to bone

testicular relating to the testicles (balls)

therapy an activity intended to help someone overcome a physical, mental, or emotional health problem

Further information

WEB SITES

www.fda.gov/Food/ResourcesForYou/Consumers/KidsTeens/default.htm
Guidance on nutrition and food safety for teens.

www.bcm.edu/cnrc/bodycomp/bmiz2.html
Calculate your BMI (specific calculator for young people).

teenshealth.org/teen/
Advice on all aspects of teenage health and fitness.

www.youngwomenshealth.org/vegetarian.html
How to eat a healthy vegetarian or vegan diet.

www.teengrowth.com/
Guidance on different aspects of teen health, including lots of letters and questions from readers.

www.coolnurse.com/
Advice on many aspects of health, especially for older teens.

www.channel4embarrassingillnesses.com/video/how-to-check-yourself/
A very good site with video demonstrations of how to check breasts, testicles, and skin for cancerous changes.

HOTLINES

Childhelp USA, National Child Abuse Hotline: 800-422-4453

National Youth Crisis Hotline: 800-442-HOPE (4673)

Covenant House Hotline: 800-999-9999

Teen Line: 800-852-8336 or teenlineonline.org

National Suicide Prevention Lifeline: 1-800-273-TALK

BOOKS

Marjolijn Bijlefeld and Sharon K. Zoumbaris, *Food and You, A Guide to Healthy Habits for Teens*, Greenwood, 2008

Jeremy Daldry, *The Teenage Guy's Survival Guide: The Real Deal on Girls, Growing Up and Other Guy Stuff*, Little, Brown, 1999

Christopher Hovius, *The Best You Can Be: A Teen's Guide to Fitness and Nutrition*, Mason Crest Publishers, 2005

Tammy Nelson, *What's Eating You? A Workbook for Teens with Anorexia, Bulimia, and Other Eating Disorders*, New Harbinger Publications, 2008

Lisa M. Schab, *The Anxiety Workbook for Teens: Activities to Help You Deal with Anxiety & Worry*, New Harbinger Publications, 2008

Index